Be Child of the
Truth and Life
'Who Are and Who Were' vs.
Child of the Lie and Death
'Who Was and Now Is Not!'

Apostle Bill Amon

BE CHILD OF THE TRUTH AND LIFE 'WHO ARE AND WHO WERE' VS. CHILD OF THE LIE AND DEATH 'WHO WAS AND NOW IS NOT!'"
written by Bill Amor
1st Edition © 2025 by Bill Amor
ISBN: 979-8-9995696-2-2

Scripture quotations taken from the KING JAMES VERSION (KJV): KING JAMES VERSION, public domain.

Scripture quotations taken from the Amplified® Bible, Copyright © 1954, 1958, 1962, 1964, 1965, 1987 by The Lockman Foundation. Used by permission. All rights reserved

Contents

Summary for "Be Child of the Truth and Life
'Who Are and Who Were' vs. Child of the Lie and
Death 'Who Was and Now Is Not!'"   5

CHAPTER 1
The Eternal Dichotomy – Truth vs. Lies   15

CHAPTER 2
The Origin of Truth – God's Eternal Nature   19

CHAPTER 3
The Father of Lies – Satan's Deception   23

CHAPTER 4
Becoming Children of Truth – Faith in Christ   28

CHAPTER 5
Living in Truth – Walking in Obedience   32

CHAPTER 6
The Fruits of Truth – Evidence of Transformation   36

CHAPTER 7
The Pathway to Death – Rejecting Truth   42

CONTENTS

CHAPTER 8
*Children of Lies – Characteristics of
Spiritual Bondage*   47

CHAPTER 9
Choosing Life Over Death – A Call to Decision   52

CHAPTER 10
*Battling Deception – Standing Firm
Against Falsehoods*   57

CHAPTER 11
Victory Through Christ – Overcoming Sin and Death   62

CHAPTER 12
Eternal Destiny – Life or Death?   66

Apostle Bill's Bio: 74

Summary for Apostle Bill Amor's Book: "Be Child of the Truth and Life 'Who Are and Who Were' vs. Child of the Lie and Death 'Who Was and Now Is Not!'"

Introduction

Apostle Bill Amor's new book, *Be Child of the Truth and Life 'Who Are and Who Were' vs. Child of the Lie and Death 'Who Was and Now Is Not!'*, draws deeply from the teachings of the King James Version (KJV) Bible to explore the eternal dichotomy between truth and falsehood, life and death, righteousness and sin. The book is a spiritual guide that challenges readers to examine their lives in light of biblical truths, urging them to align with God's eternal plan as revealed through Jesus Christ.

The Central Theme: Truth vs. Lies

The title itself reflects a profound biblical contrast between two spiritual states: being a child of truth and life versus being enslaved by lies and death. This theme is rooted in Jesus' declaration in John 14:6, where He says, **"I am the way, the truth, and the life: no man cometh unto the Father, but by me."** Here, Jesus identifies Himself as the ultimate embodiment of truth and life, offering salvation to all who believe in Him.

Conversely, those who reject this truth are described as children of lies—a concept tied to Satan's nature as "a liar, and the father of it" (John 8:44). The book emphasizes that choosing to follow Christ leads to eternal life ("who are" in God's presence), while rejecting Him results in spiritual death ("who was" but is now separated from God).

Biblical Foundations

1. Children of Truth

The book explores how believers become children of truth through faith in Jesus Christ. Drawing from passages like John 1:12— **"But as many as received him, to them gave he power to become the sons of God"**—the author explains that accepting Christ transforms individuals into heirs of God's kingdom. This transformation involves living according to God's Word (John 17:17— **"Sanctify them through thy truth: thy word is truth"**), walking in obedience (John 14:15— **"If ye love me, keep my commandments"**), and bearing fruit that glorifies God.

2. Children of Lies

In contrast, those who reject Christ are described as children of lies under Satan's dominion. The book references Revelation 17:8— **"The beast that thou sawest was and is not; and shall ascend out of the bottomless pit..."**— to illustrate how deception leads people away from God into destruction. These individuals live according to worldly desires rather than divine truth (1 John 2:16), ultimately facing eternal separation from God.

Key Messages

A Call to Choose Life

Apostle Amor urges readers to make a conscious decision about their spiritual identity. Drawing inspiration from Deuteronomy 30:19— **"I have set before you life and death... therefore choose life"**, he highlights that every person must decide whether they will follow Christ or remain ensnared by sin.

Living as Children of Truth

The book provides practical guidance for living as children of truth:

- **Faith:** Believing in Jesus as Savior (Romans 10:9).

- **Obedience:** Following His commandments (John 14:21).

- **Love:** Demonstrating love for others as evidence of discipleship (John 13:35).

Warning Against Deception

Finally, Apostle Amor warns against falling prey to false teachings or worldly distractions that lead away from God's path. He cites Matthew 7:15— **"Beware of false prophets..."**, encouraging vigilance against anything contrary to Scripture.

12 Chapters for Apostle Bill Amor's Book: "Be Child of the Truth and Life 'Who Are and Who Were' vs. Child of the Lie and Death 'Who Was and Now Is Not!'"

Chapter 1: The Eternal Dichotomy – Truth vs. Lies

This chapter introduces the central theme of the book, exploring the biblical contrast between truth and lies as revealed in Scripture. It examines foundational verses such as John 14:6, where Jesus declares Himself to be "the way, the truth, and the life," and John 8:44, which identifies Satan as "a liar, and the father of it." The chapter sets the stage for understanding how these opposing forces shape human destiny.

Chapter 2: The Origin of Truth – God's Eternal Nature

In this chapter, Apostle Amor delves into God's nature as the ultimate source of truth. Drawing from passages like Numbers 23:19 ("God is not a man, that he should lie") and Psalm 119:160 ("Thy word is true from the beginning"), readers are guided to see how God's unchanging character forms the foundation for all truth.

Chapter 3: The Father of Lies – Satan's Deception

This chapter focuses on Satan's role as the originator of lies and deception. Using Genesis 3 (the fall of man) as a case study, it explores how Satan introduced sin into humanity by distorting God's Word. Revelation 12:9 ("that old serpent, called the Devil, and Satan, which deceiveth the whole world") is also examined to highlight his ongoing influence.

Chapter 4: Becoming Children of Truth – Faith in Christ

Here, Apostle Amor explains how individuals become children of truth through faith in Jesus Christ. Key verses include John 1:12 ("But as many as received him..."), Romans 10:9-10 (confession and belief in Christ), and Ephesians 2:8-9 (salvation by grace through faith). This chapter emphasizes that salvation is a gift from God.

Chapter 5: Living in Truth – Walking in Obedience

This chapter provides practical guidance for living as children of truth by walking in obedience to God's Word. Passages like John 14:15 ("If ye love me, keep my commandments") and James 1:22 ("Be ye doers of the word") are explored to encourage believers to align their lives with biblical principles.

Chapter 6: The Fruits of Truth – Evidence of Transformation

Apostle Amor discusses how living in truth produces spiritual fruit that glorifies God. Galatians 5:22-23 (the fruit of the Spirit) serves as a key text here. This chapter also highlights how transformed lives serve as testimonies to others about God's power.

Chapter 7: The Pathway to Death – Rejecting Truth

This chapter examines what it means to reject truth and live under deception. Using Romans 1:18-32 (God giving people over to their sinful desires) as a framework, it shows how rejecting God leads to spiritual death.

Chapter 8: Children of Lies – Characteristics of Spiritual Bondage

Apostle Amor outlines characteristics that define those who live under Satan's dominion. Drawing from Ephesians 2:1-3 (walking according to "the prince of the power of the air") and Revelation 17:8 ("The beast that thou sawest was, and is not"), this chapter warns against being ensnared by worldly desires.

Chapter 9: Choosing Life Over Death – A Call to Decision

This pivotal chapter challenges readers to make a conscious decision about their spiritual identity. Deuteronomy 30:19 ("I have set before you life and death... therefore choose life") serves as an anchor verse for urging readers toward repentance and faith in Christ.

Chapter 10: Battling Deception – Standing Firm Against Falsehoods

Here, Apostle Amor equips readers with tools for resisting deception. Ephesians 6:10-18 (the armor of God) is explored in detail alongside Matthew 7:15 ("Beware of false prophets"). Practical advice is given on discerning truth from errors using Scripture.

Chapter 11: Victory Through Christ – Overcoming Sin and Death

This chapter celebrates Jesus' victory over sin and death through His resurrection. Key texts include Romans 6:23 ("For the wages of sin is death; but the gift of God is eternal life through Jesus Christ our Lord") and Revelation 21:4 (God wiping away all tears). Readers are encouraged to live victoriously in Christ.

Chapter 12: Eternal Destiny – Life or Death?

The final chapter concludes with an exploration of eternal destinies based on one's choice between truth or lies. Revelation chapters 20-22 are used to contrast eternal life with God versus eternal separation from Him in hellfire. The book ends with an urgent call for readers to embrace Jesus Christ as their Savior while there is still time.

Introduction for Apostle Bill Amor's Book: "Be Child of the Truth and Life 'Who Are and Who Were' vs. Child of the Lie and Death 'Who Was and Now Is Not!'"

In a world filled with competing voices, conflicting ideologies, and ever-present distractions, the question of spiritual identity has never been more urgent. Are you a child of truth and life, walking in alignment with God's eternal plan? Or are you ensnared by lies and death, separated from the source of true life? These profound questions form the foundation of Apostle Bill Amor's transformative new book, *Be Child of the Truth and Life 'Who Are and Who Were' vs. Child of the Lie and Death 'Who Was and Now Is Not!'*

Drawing deeply from the timeless wisdom of the King James Version (KJV) Bible, this book is both a call to action and a guide for self-reflection. It challenges readers to examine their lives through the lens of Scripture, urging them to choose between two starkly different paths: one leading to eternal life in Christ Jesus, and the other to spiritual death under the dominion of sin.

The title itself encapsulates this dichotomy. The phrase "Who Are and Who Were" refers to those who have embraced God's truth through faith in Jesus Christ—those who live in His presence now ("who are") and will continue to do so eternally ("who were"). In contrast, "Who Was and Now Is Not" describes those who reject God's truth, living under deception ("who was") but ultimately facing separation from Him ("now is not").

At its heart, this book is an exploration of what it means to live as a child of truth versus a child of lies. It delves into foundational biblical principles such as salvation through Christ alone (John 14:6), sanctification by God's Word (John 17:17), obedience to His commandments (John 14:15), and vigilance against falsehoods that lead people astray (Matthew 7:15). Through these teachings, Apostle Amor provides readers with practical tools for discerning truth from deception while encouraging them to fully embrace their identity as children of God.

This journey is not merely theoretical—it is deeply personal. Each chapter invites readers into an intimate encounter with God's Word, offering insights that illuminate their spiritual condition while pointing them toward transformation through Christ. Whether you are seeking clarity about your faith or longing for deeper intimacy with God, this book serves as both a roadmap and an invitation.

As you embark on this journey through *Be Child of the Truth and Life 'Who Are and Who Were' vs. Child of the Lie and Death 'Who Was and Now Is Not!'*, prepare to be challenged, inspired, and forever changed. The stakes could not be higher—your eternal destiny hangs in the balance. Will you choose life or death? Truth or lies? The decision is yours.

Let us begin.

Chapter 1: The Eternal Dichotomy – Truth vs. Lies

The Bible presents a profound and eternal contrast between truth and lies, a dichotomy that defines the spiritual battle at the heart of human existence. This chapter introduces this central theme, exploring how Scripture reveals truth as an attribute of God Himself and lies as the defining characteristic of Satan. By examining key biblical passages, we begin to understand how these opposing forces influence human destiny and why choosing truth is essential for eternal life.

The Nature of Truth: Jesus Christ as "The Way, The Truth, and The Life"

Truth is not merely a concept or an abstract ideal in the Bible; it is personified in Jesus Christ. In John 14:6, Jesus declares, **"I am the way, the truth, and the life: no man cometh unto the Father, but by me."** This statement establishes that truth originates from God and is embodied in His Son. It also underscores that access to eternal life is only possible through a relationship with Jesus.

The phrase "the way" signifies that Jesus provides the path to salvation; "the truth" indicates His divine nature as the ultimate reality; and "the life" emphasizes that He is the source of both physical and spiritual life. These three aspects are inseparable—truth leads to life through the way provided by Christ.

Psalm 119:160 further reinforces this idea by stating, **"Thy word is true from the beginning: and every one of thy righteous judgments endureth forever."** God›s Word is eternal and unchanging, providing a foundation for those who seek to live as children of truth. To align oneself with truth means to embrace God›s Word fully and walk in obedience to His commands.

The Nature of Lies: Satan as "A Liar, and the Father of It"

In stark contrast to Jesus' embodiment of truth stands Satan, who is described in John 8:44 as **"a liar, and the father of it."** This verse highlights Satan's role as the originator of deception. From his first appearance in Genesis 3—where he deceives Eve into eating from the forbidden tree—Satan has sought to undermine God's truth by spreading lies.

Lies are inherently destructive because they distort reality and lead people away from God's purpose. Proverbs 12:22 states, **"Lying lips are abomination to the Lord: but they that deal truly are his delight."** This verse reveals God›s abhorrence for falsehoods while emphasizing His pleasure in those who live honestly.

Revelation 17:11 provides another perspective on lies when it describes deceitful powers destined for destruction: **"And the beast that was, and is not..."** This imagery reflects how lies may appear powerful or influential for a time but ultimately lack permanence or substance. Unlike God's eternal truth, which endures forever (Psalm 119:160), lies are fleeting and lead only to ruin.

The Impact on Human Destiny

The dichotomy between truth and lies has profound implications for human destiny. Those who align themselves with God's truth become children of light (Ephesians 5:8), walking in righteousness and inheriting eternal life. Conversely, those who embrace lies follow a path leading to spiritual death.

Galatians 6:7 warns believers about this reality: **"Be not deceived; God is not mocked: for whatsoever a man soweth, that shall he also reap."** Choosing deception over truth results in consequences both in this life and beyond. Revelation 21:8 lists liars among those who face judgment in «the lake which burneth with fire and brimstone,» underscoring the severity of rejecting God›s truth.

However, Scripture also offers hope for redemption through repentance. First John 1:9 assures us that if we confess our sins—including lying—God is faithful to forgive us and cleanse us from all unrighteousness.

Conclusion

This chapter lays the foundation for understanding why living as a child of truth matters so profoundly. By examining key biblical passages such as John 14:6 (Jesus as "the way, the truth, and the life")[1] alongside John 8:44 (Satan as «a liar»), we see how these opposing forces shape human destiny. Truth leads to freedom (John 8:31-32), while lies result in bondage.

As we continue exploring this theme throughout Apostle Bill Amor's book, let us remember that aligning ourselves with God's eternal truths requires intentionality—a commitment to abide in His Word (Psalm 119) while rejecting falsehoods at every turn (Proverbs 12). Only then can we fully experience what it means to be children of light walking steadfastly toward eternity with Christ.

Chapter 2: The Origin of Truth – God's Eternal Nature

In this chapter, Apostle Bill Amor explores the profound biblical truth that God Himself is the ultimate source and embodiment of truth. By examining key passages from the King James Version (KJV) Bible, readers are invited to reflect on how God's eternal and unchanging nature serves as the foundation for all truth. This chapter emphasizes that understanding God's character is essential for living a life rooted in truth and rejecting falsehood.

God's Nature as Truth

The Bible unequivocally declares that God is not only truthful but is the very essence of truth itself. Numbers 23:19 states, **"God is not a man, that he should lie; neither the son of man, that he should repent: hath he said, and shall he not do it? or hath he spoken, and shall he not make it good?"** This verse highlights two critical aspects of God›s nature: His inability to lie and His faithfulness to fulfill His promises. Unlike humans who are prone to deceit or error, God›s words are always reliable because they stem from His perfect and holy character.

Psalm 119:160 further reinforces this idea by proclaiming, **"Thy word is true from the beginning: and every one of thy righteous judgments endureth forever."** Here, we see that God's Word—His revealed truth—is eternal and unchanging. From the very beginning of creation until eternity, God's judgments remain steadfast. This consistency reflects His divine nature as immutable (unchanging) and wholly trustworthy.

The Eternality of Truth

Apostle Amor draws attention to Revelation 1:8 where God declares Himself as **"Alpha and Omega, the beginning and the ending... which is, and which was, and which is to come."** This self-identification underscores God's eternal existence—He transcends time itself. Because He exists outside of time's limitations, His truth remains constant across all generations. Unlike human philosophies or cultural norms that shift with time, God's truth endures forever.

Isaiah 40:8 echoes this sentiment by stating, **"The grass withereth, the flower fadeth: but the word of our God shall stand forever."** Just as physical things in this world decay or change over time, human ideas often fade away or prove unreliable. In contrast, God›s Word stands firm because it originates from an eternal source.

Jesus Christ as Truth Incarnate

Central to Apostle Amor's argument is Jesus Christ's declaration in John 14:6: **"I am the way, the truth, and the life: no man cometh unto the Father, but by me."** This statement reveals that truth is not merely an abstract concept but a person—Jesus Himself. As God incarnate (John 1:14), Jesus embodies divine truth in human form. Everything He taught and did reflected God's eternal nature.

In John 17:17 during His prayer for His disciples before His crucifixion, Jesus asks God to sanctify them through His Word by saying, **"Sanctify them through thy truth: thy word is truth."** This verse ties together two key ideas about God›s nature as truth:

1. Sanctification (the process of being made holy) comes through alignment with God's Word.

2. The Word itself represents absolute truth because it flows directly from God's character.

Implications for Believers

Understanding that God is the origin of all truth has profound implications for believers:

- **Trust in God's Promises:** Since God cannot lie (Titus 1:2), believers can have complete confidence in His promises. Whether it›s assurance of salvation (John 3:16) or provision during trials (Philippians 4:19), every promise in Scripture reflects God›s unwavering faithfulness.

- **Anchor in a Changing World:** In a world filled with shifting values and conflicting ideologies, believers can find stability by grounding themselves in God›s eternal truths.

- **Call to Reflect Divine Truth:** As children of God (Ephesians 5:1), Christians are called to imitate their Heavenly Father by living lives marked by honesty and integrity (Colossians 3:9).

Rejecting Falsehood

Apostle Amor contrasts this divine standard with human-ity's propensity toward deception—a trait inherited from Satan himself. John 8:44 describes Satan as **"a liar, and the father of it."** Lies originate from rebellion against God›s nature; therefore, embracing falsehood distances individuals from Him.

Proverbs 12:22 warns against dishonesty by stating that **"Lying lips are abomination to the Lord: but they that deal truly are his delight."** To live as "Children of Truth," believers must reject lies in all forms—whether they arise from personal sin or societal pressures—and instead align their lives with God's unchanging Word.

Conclusion

In "The Origin of Truth – God's Eternal Nature," Apostle Bill Amor masterfully demonstrates how understanding God's character provides clarity amidst life's uncertainties. By rec-ognizing Him as both Creator and Sustainer—the Alpha and Omega—believers can confidently build their lives upon an unshakable foundation rooted in divine truth.

Through scriptural insights such as Numbers 23:19 ("God cannot lie")[1], Psalm 119:160 ("Thy word is true"), John 14:6 ("I am...the truth"), among others cited throughout this chap-ter—readers are reminded that aligning themselves with God's eternal truths leads not only to spiritual growth but also ensures victory over deception.

Chapter 3: The Father of Lies – Satan's Deception

The Bible unequivocally identifies Satan as the originator of lies and deception. In John 8:44, Jesus declares, **"Ye are of your father the devil, and the lusts of your father ye will do. He was a murderer from the beginning, and abode not in the truth, because there is no truth in him. When he speaketh a lie, he speaketh of his own: for he is a liar, and the father of it."** This verse establishes Satan's nature as fundamentally opposed to truth. His primary weapon against humanity is deception—a tool he has wielded since the dawn of creation.

The First Lie: Genesis 3 and the Fall of Man

The first recorded instance of Satan's deception occurs in Genesis 3, where he appears in the form of a serpent to tempt Eve. This pivotal moment marks the introduction of sin into humanity through cunning manipulation and distortion of God's Word.

In Genesis 2:16-17, God gives Adam a clear command: **"Of every tree of the garden thou mayest freely eat: But of the tree of the knowledge of good and evil, thou shalt not eat of it: for in the day that thou eatest thereof thou shalt surely die."** However, when Satan approaches Eve in Genesis 3:1-5, he subtly twists God's words to sow doubt and confusion:

1. **Questioning God's Command:**
   Satan begins by asking Eve, **"Yea, hath God said, Ye shall not eat of every tree of the gar-**

den?" (Genesis 3:1). This question is designed to misrepresent God's generosity as restrictive. By framing it this way, Satan plants seeds of doubt about God's intentions.

2. **Contradicting God's Warning:**
   After Eve explains that eating from the forbidden tree would result in death (Genesis 3:2-3), Satan directly contradicts her by saying, **"Ye shall not surely die"** (Genesis 3:4). Here we see Satan blatantly denying God's truth—a hallmark characteristic of his deceptive nature.

3. **Promising False Enlightenment:**
   Finally, Satan entices Eve with a promise that eating from the tree will make her like God: **"For God doth know that in the day ye eat thereof, then your eyes shall be opened, and ye shall be as gods, knowing good and evil"** (Genesis 3:5). This appeal to pride and self-exaltation ultimately leads Eve— and subsequently Adam—to disobey God.

Through this account in Genesis 3, we see how Satan uses lies to undermine trust in God's Word. His strategy involves questioning divine authority, distorting truth with partial truths or outright falsehoods, and appealing to human desires for autonomy and power.

Revelation 12:9 – The Ongoing Influence of Deception

Satan's role as "the father of lies" extends far beyond Eden. Revelation 12:9 provides a vivid description of his ongoing influence over humanity throughout history: **"And the great**

dragon was cast out, that old serpent, called the Devil, and Satan, which deceiveth the whole world."

This verse connects back to Genesis by referring to Satan as "that old serpent," emphasizing his continuity as a deceiver from Eden onward. It also highlights his global impact—Satan does not merely deceive individuals but works on a grand scale to lead entire nations astray.

Examples abound throughout Scripture where Satan employs deception:

- In Job 1-2, he accuses Job before God in an attempt to undermine Job's faithfulness.

- In Matthew 4:1-11 during Jesus' temptation in the wilderness, Satan misuses Scripture itself to try to lead Jesus into sin.

- Second Corinthians 11:14 warns believers that **"Satan himself is transformed into an angel of light,"** demonstrating his ability to disguise evil as good.

These examples underscore how pervasive and insidious Satan's deceptions are—they infiltrate every aspect of human life when left unchecked.

The Consequences of Believing Lies

The consequences for Adam and Eve after succumbing to

Satan's lies were immediate and severe:

1. They experienced spiritual death—separation from God's presence (Genesis 3:23-24).

2. They became aware of their nakedness and felt shame for the first time (Genesis 3:7).

3. Humanity inherited sinfulness: Romans 5:12 explains that through Adam's disobedience sin entered into all mankind.

Similarly today, believing lies instead of God's truth leads people away from salvation toward destruction. Proverbs 14:12 warns us that **"There is a way which seemeth right unto a man, but the end thereof are ways unto death."**

Overcoming Deception Through Truth

While this chapter focuses on exposing Satan's deceptive tactics as "the father of lies," it also points readers toward victory through God's truth:

- Jesus Christ declared Himself as "the way," "the truth," and "the life" (John 14:6), offering freedom from bondage through faith.

- Ephesians 6 describes spiritual armor believers must wear against deception, including "the belt" symbolizing truth (Ephesians 6:14).

- Psalm119 reminds us repeatedly about meditating upon scripture daily being key combatting deceitful influences around us constantly surrounding modern society globally alike!

By anchoring ourselves firmly within biblical teachings trusting Holy Spirit guidance discernment prayerful reflection daily basis ensures protection against falling prey enemy schemes traps laid path journey eternal kingdom heaven above!

Chapter 4: Becoming Children of Truth – Faith in Christ

In this pivotal chapter, Apostle Bill Amor delves into the transformative process by which individuals become "Children of Truth" through faith in Jesus Christ. Drawing from the King James Version (KJV) Bible, he emphasizes that this transformation is not achieved by human effort or merit but is a divine gift of grace, accessible to all who believe and receive Christ as their Savior. This chapter explores the foundational truths of salvation, highlighting key biblical passages that illuminate the path to becoming a child of truth.

Receiving Christ: The First Step Toward Truth

The journey to becoming a child of truth begins with receiving Jesus Christ. John 1:12 declares:
"But as many as received him, to them gave he power to become the sons of God, even to them that believe on his name."

This verse underscores two essential components: receiving and believing. To "receive" Christ means to welcome Him into one's life as Lord and Savior, acknowledging His authority and surrendering fully to His will. Believing "on His name" signifies placing complete trust in who Jesus is—the Son of God—and what He has accomplished through His death and resurrection.

Apostle Amor explains that this act of receiving and believing is not merely intellectual assent but a heartfelt commitment. It involves recognizing one's need for salvation due to sin (Romans 3:23) and turning away from self-reliance toward dependence on God's grace.

Confession and Belief: The Heart of Salvation

Romans 10:9-10 provides further clarity on how individuals become children of truth through faith in Christ:
"That if thou shalt confess with thy mouth the Lord Jesus, and shalt believe in thine heart that God hath raised him from the dead, thou shalt be saved. For with the heart man believeth unto righteousness; and with the mouth confession is made unto salvation."

Here, Apostle Amor highlights two critical actions required for salvation:

1. **Confession:** Openly declaring Jesus as Lord signifies a public acknowledgment of His lordship over one's life. This confession is not merely verbal but reflects an inner conviction.

2. **Belief:** Genuine faith resides in the heart—a deep-seated trust in God's redemptive work through Christ's resurrection.

Apostle Amor emphasizes that these two elements—confession and belief—are inseparable. True faith manifests outwardly through confession while being rooted inwardly in heartfelt belief.

Salvation by Grace Through Faith

One of the most profound truths about becoming a child of truth is that salvation is entirely a gift from God. Ephesians 2:8-9 states:
"For by grace are ye saved through faith; and that not of yourselves: it is the gift of God: Not of works, lest any man should boast."

Apostle Amor explains that grace refers to God's unmerited favor—His willingness to save sinners despite their unworthiness. Faith, on the other hand, is the means by which individuals receive this grace. Importantly, neither grace nor faith originates from human effort; both are gifts bestowed by God.

This passage also dismantles any notion that good works can earn salvation. As Apostle Amor notes, attempting to achieve righteousness through deeds leads only to pride and self-reliance rather than humble dependence on God.

The Transformative Power of Faith

Faith in Christ does more than secure eternal life—it transforms believers into new creations (2 Corinthians 5:17). Apostle Amor draws attention to how this transformation aligns believers with truth:

- **Adoption into God's Family:** Through faith, believers are adopted as children of God (Galatians 4:5-7), gaining access to His promises and inheritance.

- **Freedom from Sin:** John 8:32 proclaims, «And ye shall know the truth, and the truth shall make you free.» Faith liberates believers from bondage to sin by aligning them with God›s eternal truth.

- **Empowerment for Righteous Living:** As children of truth, believers are empowered by the Holy Spirit to walk in obedience (Galatians 5:16).

Conclusion

In this chapter, Apostle Bill Amor masterfully articulates how individuals become children of truth through faith in Jesus Christ. By receiving Him as Lord and Savior (John 1:12), confessing Him openly while believing deeply (Romans 10:9-10), and embracing salvation as a gift of grace (Ephesians 2:8-9), believers are transformed into new creations aligned with God's eternal truth.

This process underscores an essential biblical principle— that salvation is not earned but freely given by a loving God who desires all people to come into His light (1 Timothy 2:4). As Apostle Amor concludes this chapter, he challenges readers to reflect on their own spiritual journey and invites them to take hold of this incredible gift by placing their faith wholly in Christ.

Chapter 5: Living in Truth – Walking in Obedience

Living as children of truth requires more than mere acknowledgment of God's Word; it demands active obedience. The Bible consistently emphasizes that true faith is demonstrated through actions, not just words. In this chapter, we will explore how walking in obedience to God's commandments enables believers to live in truth and reflect the character of Christ. By examining key passages from the King James Version (KJV) Bible, we will uncover practical steps for aligning our lives with biblical principles.

The Foundation of Obedience: Love for God

Obedience to God begins with love. Jesus Himself declared in John 14:15, **"If ye love me, keep my commandments."** This verse establishes a direct connection between love and obedience. To truly love God is to honor His Word and follow His instructions. It is not enough to profess faith verbally; our actions must align with our declarations.

The Apostle John reiterates this principle in 1 John 5:3: **"For this is the love of God, that we keep his commandments: and his commandments are not grievous."** Here, we see that obedience is not meant to be burdensome but rather a joyful expression of our devotion to God. When we understand that His commands are given for our benefit and protection, we can embrace them wholeheartedly.

Being Doers of the Word

James 1:22 provides a powerful exhortation for believers: **"But be ye doers of the word, and not hearers only, deceiving your own selves."** This verse warns against self-deception—a danger faced by those who hear God's Word but fail to act upon it. True discipleship requires putting faith into practice.

Jesus illustrated this concept through the parable of the wise and foolish builders in Matthew 7:24-27. He compared those who hear His words and obey them to a wise man who built his house upon a rock. Conversely, those who hear but do not obey are likened to a foolish man whose house collapses during storms.[4] This parable underscores the importance of building our lives on the solid foundation of obedience.

Walking in Truth Through Righteous Living

To walk in truth means living righteously according to God's standards. Ephesians 4:25 instructs believers to **"put away lying"** and instead speak truthfully with one another. Similarly, Colossians 3:9-10 urges Christians to **"lie not one to another"** but rather embrace their renewed identity in Christ.

Walking in truth also involves rejecting sin and pursuing holiness. Romans 6:16 reminds us that obedience determines whom we serve: **"Know ye not, that to whom ye yield yourselves servants to obey, his servants ye**

are... whether of sin unto death, or of obedience unto righteousness?" By choosing righteousness over sin, we demonstrate our commitment to living as children of truth.

Practical Steps for Walking in Obedience

1. **Study God's Word Regularly:** Psalm 119:105 declares, **"Thy word is a lamp unto my feet, and a light unto my path."** Immersing ourselves in Scripture equips us with the knowledge needed for righteous living.

2. **Pray for Guidance:** Proverbs 3:5-6 encourages believers to trust in the Lord and seek His direction: **"Trust in the Lord with all thine heart; and lean not unto thine own understanding. In all thy ways acknowledge him, and he shall direct thy paths."**

3. **Rely on the Holy Spirit:** Galatians 5:16 advises us to walk by the Spirit so that we do not fulfill sinful desires. The Holy Spirit empowers us to live obediently.

4. **Confess and Repent:** When we fall short, 1 John 1:9 assures us that if we confess our sins, God is faithful to forgive us.

5. **Surround Yourself with Fellow Believers:** Hebrews 10:24-25 highlights the importance of fellowship for mutual encouragement.

The Blessings of Obedience

Obedience brings blessings both now and eternally. Deuteronomy 28 outlines numerous blessings promised to those who diligently obey God's commands—prosperity, protection, and favor among them. Furthermore, Jesus assures us in John 15:10-11 that abiding in His love through obedience leads to fullness of joy.

Ultimately, walking in obedience allows us to reflect Christ's character and glorify God through our lives (Matthew 5:16). As children of truth who live according to His Word, we become lights shining brightly in a world darkened by deception.

Conclusion

Living as children of truth requires intentionality—choosing daily to walk obediently according to God's Word out of love for Him. By being doers rather than mere hearers of Scripture (James 1:22), rejecting falsehood (Ephesians 4:25), pursuing righteousness (Romans 6:16), and relying on divine guidance (Proverbs 3:5-6), believers can align their lives with biblical principles.

As Apostle Bill Amor emphasizes throughout this book's message rooted deeply within Scripture itself—truth endures eternally while lies fade away into nothingness (Revelation 21). Let us therefore commit ourselves wholly unto Him who is Truth incarnate!

Chapter 6: The Fruits of Truth – Evidence of Transformation

In this chapter, Apostle Bill Amor delves into the transformative power of living in truth and how it manifests as spiritual fruit in the lives of believers. Drawing from the King James Version (KJV) Bible, he emphasizes that a life rooted in God's truth is not only personally fulfilling but also serves as a testimony to others about the power and glory of God. The key text for this chapter is **Galatians 5:22-23**, which outlines the "fruit of the Spirit"—the evidence of a life transformed by walking in alignment with God's truth.

The Fruit of the Spirit: A Reflection of Truth

The Apostle Paul writes in **Galatians 5:22-23**:

"But the fruit of the Spirit is love, joy, peace, long suffering, gentleness, goodness, faith, meekness, temperance: against such there is no law."

Apostle Amor explains that these nine attributes are not merely virtues to aspire to; they are evidence of a life that has been fundamentally changed by God's truth. When someone becomes a "Child of Truth," their character begins to reflect these qualities because they are no longer living according to their sinful nature but are instead led by the Holy Spirit. This transformation is not superficial or temporary; it is deep and enduring.

Each aspect of the fruit of the Spirit represents a dimension of God's character:

- **Love**: The selfless and unconditional love that mirrors God's love for humanity (1 John 4:8).

- **Joy**: A deep-seated gladness that transcends circumstances (Psalm 16:11).

- **Peace**: An inner calm and assurance rooted in trust in God (Philippians 4:7).

- **Longsuffering** (Patience): Endurance through trials without complaint (Colossians 1:11).

- **Gentleness**: Kindness and compassion toward others (Ephesians 4:32).

- **Goodness**: Moral integrity and generosity (Romans 15:14).

- **Faith** (Faithfulness): Steadfast loyalty and trustworthiness (Hebrews 11:1).

- **Meekness** (Humility): Strength under control; submission to God's will (Matthew 5:5).

- **Temperance** (Self-Control): Mastery over one's desires and impulses through reliance on the Holy Spirit (2 Timothy 1:7).

These fruits are not produced by human effort alone but are cultivated by abiding in Christ. As Jesus said in **John 15:5**, *"I am the vine, ye are the branches... for without me ye can do nothing."* Living in truth requires staying connected to Christ through prayer, studying Scripture, and obedience.

Evidence of Transformation

Apostle Amor underscores that when believers live out these fruits, their lives become powerful testimonies to others about God's transformative power. In Matthew 7:16-20, Jesus teaches that people will be recognized by their fruits:

"Ye shall know them by their fruits... Every good tree bringeth forth good fruit; but a corrupt tree bringeth forth evil fruit."

This passage highlights an important principle—true transformation cannot be hidden. Just as a healthy tree naturally produces good fruit, so too does a life grounded in God's truth naturally bear spiritual fruit. This visible change serves as evidence to others that God's Word is alive and active.

For example:

- A person who once struggled with anger may now exhibit patience and gentleness.

- Someone who lived selfishly may now demonstrate sacrificial love.

- An individual plagued by anxiety may now radiate peace.

These changes are not merely behavioral modifications but reflect an inward renewal brought about by the Holy Spirit (**2 Corinthians 5:17**). As Apostle Amor notes, such transformations glorify God because they point back to His power at work within us.

Transformed Lives as Testimonies

Living as a "Child of Truth" means becoming a beacon for others who are searching for hope and meaning. In Matthew 5:14-16, Jesus calls His followers *"the light of the world"* and urges them to let their light shine before men so that others may see their good works and glorify God. Apostle Amor highlights this passage as central to understanding how transformed lives serve as testimonies.

When believers embody truth through their actions—whether it's showing kindness to strangers, forgiving those who wrong them, or standing firm in faith during trials—they draw others toward Christ. Their lives become living epistles (**2 Corinthians 3:2-3**) read by all who encounter them.

Furthermore, Apostle Amor points out that bearing spiritual fruit often opens doors for evangelism. When people witness genuine transformation, especially when it occurs against all odds, they become curious about its source. This curiosity provides opportunities for believers to share their faith boldly yet humbly (**1 Peter 3:15**).

Challenges Along the Way

While bearing spiritual fruit brings glory to God and impacts others positively, it is not without challenges. Apostle Amor acknowledges that believers face opposition from both external forces (e.g., persecution) and internal struggles (e.g., battling old habits). However, he reminds readers that perseverance is key:

"And let us not be weary in well doing: for in due season we shall reap if we faint not." (**Galatians 6:9**)

By relying on God's strength rather than their own efforts (**Philippians 4:13**), believers can overcome obstacles and continue producing fruit even during difficult seasons.

Conclusion

In conclusion, Chapter 6 emphasizes that living in truth produces tangible evidence—a harvest of spiritual fruit—that glorifies God while serving as a testimony to others. By abiding in Christ and allowing His Word to shape their lives, believers can reflect His character through love, joy, peace, patience, kindness, goodness, faithfulness, humility, and self-control. These fruits not only enrich personal relationships but also draw others closer to God.

Apostle Bill Amor encourages readers to examine their own lives honestly—are they bearing good fruit? If so, they can rejoice knowing they are walking as "Children of Truth." If it is not yet evident or consistent enough, due perhaps still to wrestling with old patterns, then take heart because the process of sanctification is an ongoing journey yielding evermore abundant harvest over time, by faithful surrender and daily renewal, unto the Lordship of our Savior and Redeemer King Eternal!

Chapter 7: The Pathway to Death – Rejecting Truth

The Bible is clear that rejecting truth and embracing deception leads to spiritual death. This chapter delves into the consequences of turning away from God's truth, using Romans 1:18-32 as a foundational passage. The Apostle Paul outlines how humanity's rejection of God results in a downward spiral into sin, corruption, and ultimately, separation from God. By examining this passage and other supporting scriptures from the King James Version (KJV) Bible, we will uncover the dangers of rejecting truth and living under deception.

The Suppression of Truth

Romans 1:18 begins with a sobering statement:
"For the wrath of God is revealed from heaven against all ungodliness and unrighteousness of men, who hold the truth in unrighteousness."

This verse establishes that God's wrath is directed toward those who suppress the truth through their unrighteous actions. To "hold the truth in unrighteousness" means to possess knowledge of God's truth but choose to reject or distort it for selfish purposes. Humanity has no excuse for this rejection because, as Paul explains in Romans 1:19-20:
"Because that which may be known of God is manifest in them; for God hath shewed it unto them. For the invisible things of him from the creation of the world are clearly seen, being understood by the things that are made, even his eternal power and Godhead; so that they are without excuse."

God has revealed Himself through creation—His power, divine nature, and existence are evident in everything He has made. Yet many choose to ignore this revelation, suppressing what they know to be true about God.

Rejecting this fundamental truth about God's existence is the first step on the pathway to spiritual death. It begins with a refusal to acknowledge Him as Creator and Sovereign Lord.

Idolatry: Replacing Truth with Lies

When people reject God's truth, they inevitably replace it with lies. Romans 1:21-23 describes this tragic exchange: *"Because that, when they knew God, they glorified him not as God, neither were thankful; but became vain in their imaginations, and their foolish heart was darkened. Professing themselves to be wise, they became fools, And changed the glory of the uncorruptible God into an image made like to corruptible man..."*

Instead of worshipping the Creator, humanity turns to idolatry—worshipping created things rather than God Himself. This idolatry can take many forms: materialism (worshipping wealth), humanism (exalting human intellect above divine wisdom), or even literal idol worship (as seen throughout history). These false gods cannot save or satisfy because they are rooted in lies rather than eternal truth.

Psalm 115:4-8 vividly describes idols as lifeless objects incapable of action or thought:

"Their idols are silver and gold, the work of men's hands... They have mouths, but they speak not: eyes have they, but they see not... They that make them are like unto them; so is everyone that trusteth in them."

By rejecting God's truth and embracing idolatry or falsehoods instead, people cut themselves off from His life-giving presence.

The Consequences of Rejecting Truth

Romans 1:24-28 outlines what happens when people persistently reject God's truth—they are "given over" by Him to their sinful desires:

1. **Impurity:**
   "Wherefore God also gave them up to uncleanness through the lusts of their own hearts..." (Romans 1:24)
   When people reject God's moral standards, He allows them to pursue their sinful passions unchecked. This leads to moral decay and dishonor within themselves.

2. **Idolatrous Worship:**
   "Who changed the truth of God into a lie..." (Romans 1:25)
   People exchange God's eternal truths for lies that justify their sinful behavior.

3. **Degrading Passions:**
   "For this cause God gave them up unto vile affections..." (Romans 1:26)

As society moves further away from God's design for relationships and morality, unnatural desires become normalized.

4. **A Depraved Mind:**
   "And even as they did not like to retain God in their knowledge, God gave them over to a reprobate mind..." (Romans 1:28)
   A "reprobate mind" refers to a conscience so seared by sin that it can no longer discern right from wrong.

These consequences illustrate how rejecting God's truth leads individuals—and entire societies—into deeper levels of corruption and depravity.

Spiritual Death as Final Judgment

The ultimate result of rejecting truth is spiritual death—eternal separation from God. Romans 6:23 warns us plainly: *"For the wages of sin is death; but the gift of God is eternal life through Jesus Christ our Lord."*

Revelation 21:8 provides further clarity on this judgment for those who live under deception rather than embracing God's truth: *"But the fearful, and unbelieving...and all liars shall have their part in the lake which burneth with fire and brimstone..."*

This eternal punishment underscores why rejecting God's truth is so dangerous—it leads not only to destruction in this life but also eternal separation from His presence.

Hope Through Repentance

Despite these dire warnings about rejecting truth, there remains hope for redemption through repentance. Second Peter 3:9 reminds us: *"The Lord is...not willing that any should perish but that all should come to repentance."*

No matter how far someone has strayed down this pathway toward spiritual death by rejecting God's truths or living under deception—they can still turn back toward Him through faith in Jesus Christ.

As Jesus declared in John 14:6: *"I am the way—the TRUTH—and life!"*

By accepting Christ's sacrifice on behalf sinners & submitting fully unto His lordship believers find freedom salvation reconciliation w/ Almighty Creator!

In Conclusion, Chapter Seven serves both warning encouragement readers avoid pitfalls associated w/ rejecting divine truths embrace transformative power gospel message!

Chapter 8: Children of Lies – Characteristics of Spiritual Bondage

Apostle Bill Amor, in his profound exploration of spiritual truths, dedicates this chapter to identifying the characteristics of those who live under the dominion of lies and deception. Drawing heavily from the King James Version (KJV) Bible, he warns against the spiritual bondage that results from aligning oneself with Satan, "the prince of the power of the air" (Ephesians 2:2) and succumbing to worldly desires. This chapter serves as both a cautionary tale and a guide for believers to recognize and avoid these pitfalls.

The Nature of Spiritual Bondage

The Bible describes spiritual bondage as a state where individuals are enslaved by sin and separated from God. In Ephesians 2:1-3, Paul writes:

"And you hath he quickened, who were dead in trespasses and sins; Wherein in time past ye walked according to the course of this world, according to the prince of the power of the air, the spirit that now worketh in the children of disobedience: Among whom also we all had our conversation in times past in the lusts of our flesh, fulfilling the desires of the flesh and of the mind; and were by nature the children of wrath, even as others."

This passage highlights several key characteristics that define those living under spiritual bondage:

1. **Dead in Trespasses and Sins**
   Those who are spiritually dead are separated from God due to their sins. Sin creates a barrier between humanity and God's holiness (Isaiah 59:2). Apostle Amor emphasizes that this state is not merely about committing individual acts of sin but living in a continual pattern of rebellion against God.

2. **Walking According to "the Prince of the Power of the Air"**
   Satan is described as "the prince of the power of the air," signifying his influence over worldly systems and those who reject God's authority. This phrase underscores how Satan manipulates human desires through temptations such as pride, greed, lust, and envy. Revelation 17:8 further illustrates this concept with its description of "the beast that thou sawest was, and is not," symbolizing fleeting powers that deceive humanity but ultimately lead to destruction.

3. **Children of Disobedience**
   Those under Satan's dominion are referred to as "children of disobedience." This term reflects their willful rejection of God's commandments and their alignment with sinful behaviors. As Jesus said in John 8:44: *"Ye are of your father the devil, and the lusts of your father ye will do."* Apostle Amor warns readers that disobedience leads to deeper entanglement in lies.

4. **Fulfilling Desires of Flesh and Mind**
   Spiritual bondage manifests through an unrestrained pursuit of carnal pleasures—whether physical or intellectual—that oppose God's will. Galatians 5:19-21 lists works of the flesh such as adultery, idolatry,

hatred, strife, envyings, drunkenness, and revelings. These behaviors enslave individuals by feeding their sinful nature rather than nurturing their spirit.

5. **Children by Nature Under Wrath**
   Finally, Paul describes those living apart from Christ as being "by nature children of wrath." This means they are subject to God's righteous judgment because they have chosen rebellion over submission to His truth.

The Deceptive Allurements Leading to Bondage

Apostle Amor elaborates on how worldly desires act as snares that trap individuals into spiritual bondage:

- **Materialism:** The relentless pursuit of wealth blinds people to eternal values (Matthew 6:24).

- **Pride:** A self-centered focus leads individuals away from humility before God (Proverbs 16:18).

- **False Teachings:** Deceptive doctrines distort biblical truths (2 Timothy 4:3-4).

Revelation 17 provides a vivid depiction through its imagery concerning Babylon—a symbol for corrupt systems driven by greed and immorality.[5] Verse 8 warns about deceptive powers like «the beast,» which appear dominant but ultimately «go into perdition.»

Breaking Free from Spiritual Bondage

While this chapter focuses on identifying characteristics associated with spiritual enslavement, Apostle Amor also offers hope for deliverance through Christ:

1. **Repentance:** Turning away from sin is essential for breaking free from bondage (Acts 3:19).

2. **Faith in Christ:** Only Jesus can set captives free (John 8:36). Believers must trust Him fully for salvation.

3. **Renewal Through Scripture:** Immersing oneself in God›s Word transforms minds (Romans 12:2).

4. **Walking by Spirit:** Living according to Holy Spirit guidance ensures victory over fleshly desires (Galatians 5:16).

Conclusion

In conclusion, Apostle Bill Amor's Chapter 8 serves as both a warning against falling prey to Satan's deceptions and an encouragement for believers seeking freedom through Christ. By recognizing these characteristics—spiritual death due to sinfulness; walking under Satanic influence; disobedience; indulgence in fleshly desires; being subject to divine wrath—readers can better understand what it means to live outside God's truth versus embracing His eternal light.

As Revelation reminds us repeatedly throughout its prophetic visions—the forces aligned with falsehood may seem powerful temporarily but are destined for ultimate defeat when confronted by God's eternal truth.

Chapter 9: Choosing Life Over Death – A Call to Decision

The Bible is clear that every individual faces a choice between two paths: life or death, truth or falsehood, light or darkness. This pivotal chapter calls readers to examine their spiritual identity and make a conscious decision about whom they will serve. The foundation of this call is rooted in **Deuteronomy 30:19**, where Moses declares to the Israelites:

"I call heaven and earth to record this day against you, that I have set before you life and death, blessing and cursing: therefore choose life, that both thou and thy seed may live."

This verse encapsulates the heart of God's desire for humanity—to choose life by aligning with His truth and rejecting the lies of sin and deception. In this chapter, we will explore what it means to choose life over death, the consequences of each choice, and how one can walk steadfastly in the path of eternal life.

The Choice Between Life and Death

From the very beginning of creation, God has given humanity free will—the ability to choose between obedience to Him (life) or rebellion against Him (death). In Genesis 2:16-17, God commanded Adam not to eat from the tree of the knowledge of good and evil:

"And the Lord God commanded the man, saying, Of every

tree of the garden thou mayest freely eat: But of the tree of the knowledge of good and evil, thou shalt not eat of it: for in the day that thou eatest thereof thou shalt surely die."

This command highlights a fundamental principle: obedience leads to life while disobedience results in separation from God—spiritual death. Unfortunately, Adam and Eve chose rebellion when they believed Satan's lie (Genesis 3:4-5), introducing sin into the world. Since then, all humanity has been faced with this same choice.

In Deuteronomy 30:15-16, Moses reiterates this principle as he addresses Israel before they enter the Promised Land:

"See, I have set before thee this day life and good, and death and evil; In that I command thee this day to love the Lord thy God, to walk in his ways..."

Choosing life involves loving God wholeheartedly, obeying His commandments, and walking in His ways. It is not merely an intellectual decision but a commitment that transforms one's entire being.

The Blessings of Choosing Life

In contrast to death's destruction are abundant blessings for those who choose life by following Christ. Jesus Himself declared:

"I am come that they might have life, and that they might have it more abundantly." (John 10:10)

This abundant life begins now as believers experience peace with God (Romans 5:1), joy through His Spirit (Galatians 5:22), and purpose in serving Him (Ephesians 2:10). Most importantly, choosing life secures eternal fellowship with God:

"And this is life eternal, that they might know thee the only true God, and Jesus Christ..." (John 17:3)

The blessings extend beyond individuals; Deuteronomy 30:19 emphasizes generational impact—"that both thou and thy seed may live." When parents model faithfulness to God's truth, they leave a legacy for their children.

How to Choose Life

To choose life requires repentance—a turning away from sin—and faith in Jesus Christ as Savior. Acts 3:19 urges:

"Repent ye therefore, and be converted, that your sins may be blotted out..."

Jesus' sacrifice on Calvary makes it possible for sinners to be reconciled with God. As Romans 10:9 explains:

"That if thou shalt confess with thy mouth the Lord Jesus, and shalt believe in thine heart that God hath raised him from the dead, thou shalt be saved."

Choosing life also involves daily surrender—denying one-self to follow Christ fully (Luke 9:23). It means abiding in His Word (John 8:31-32), walking by faith rather than sight (2 Corinthians 5:7), and relying on His strength rather than one's own efforts.

A Call to Decision

As you read these words today—just as Moses called Israel centuries ago—you are faced with a choice. Will you align yourself with truth or deception? Will you embrace eternal life through Christ or cling to fleeting pleasures that lead only to destruction?

God pleads through Scripture for every person to choose wisely because He desires none should perish but all come unto repentance (2 Peter 3:9). The decision is yours alone; no one else can make it for you.

Let these words resonate deeply within your heart:

"Choose you this day whom ye will serve...but as for me and my house we will serve the Lord." (Joshua 24:15)

May today be your moment of decision—a turning point where you reject lies forevermore while embracing Truth Himself—Jesus Christ.

Chapter 10: Battling Deception – Standing Firm Against Falsehoods

In this pivotal chapter, Apostle Bill Amor delves into the spiritual battle that every believer must face: resisting deception and standing firm in God's truth. Drawing from the King James Version (KJV) Bible, he equips readers with biblical tools and practical advice to discern truth from error. The chapter emphasizes the importance of spiritual vigilance, reliance on Scripture, and the application of God's armor as outlined in Ephesians 6:10-18.

The Reality of Deception

Deception is not a new phenomenon; it has been present since the Garden of Eden when Satan deceived Eve (Genesis 3:1-6). Jesus Himself warned His followers about the prevalence of falsehoods in Matthew 7:15: **"Beware of false prophets, which come to you in sheep's clothing, but inwardly they are ravening wolves."** This verse highlights how deception often masquerades as truth, making it all the more dangerous. False prophets and teachers may appear righteous outwardly but lead others astray with distorted doctrines or self-serving motives.

Apostle Amor underscores that believers must remain vigilant because deception can infiltrate even within the church. As Paul warns in 2 Corinthians 11:13-15, Satan disguises himself as an angel of light, and his servants do likewise. Therefore, Christians must be equipped to recognize and resist these tactics.

The Armor of God: A Divine Defense Against Deception

To stand firm against falsehoods, Apostle Amor turns to Ephesians 6:10-18—the passage on the armor of God. Here, Paul provides a metaphorical depiction of spiritual warfare and outlines six essential pieces of armor that enable believers to withstand deception:

1. **The Belt of Truth (Ephesians 6:14):** The belt secures all other pieces of armor and represents integrity and commitment to God's truth. Jesus declared in John 17:17, **"Sanctify them through thy truth: thy word is truth."** By grounding oneself in Scripture, believers can discern lies and hold fast to what is true.

2. **The Breastplate of Righteousness (Ephesians 6:14):** Righteousness protects the heart—the seat of emotions and will—against corruption. Proverbs 4:23 reminds us to guard our hearts diligently because they influence every aspect of life.

3. **The Shoes of the Gospel of Peace (Ephesians 6:15):** Just as sturdy footwear enables soldiers to march confidently into battle, readiness rooted in the gospel allows believers to stand firm amid challenges. Isaiah 52:7 celebrates those who bring good news with peace.

4. **The Shield of Faith (Ephesians 6:16):** Faith acts as a shield that extinguishes fiery darts—doubts, temptations, or accusations—from the enemy. Hebrews 11 defines faith as confidence in what we

hope for and assurance about what we do not see.

5. **The Helmet of Salvation (Ephesians 6:17):** Protecting one's mind is crucial in resisting deception. Romans 12:2 urges believers not to conform to worldly patterns but to renew their minds through God's Word.

6. **The Sword of the Spirit (Ephesians 6:17):** Unlike defensive armor pieces, this weapon actively combats lies by wielding God's Word effectively. When tempted by Satan in Matthew 4:1-11, Jesus countered each lie with Scripture—a model for all believers.

Finally, Paul emphasizes prayer as an overarching strategy for spiritual warfare (Ephesians 6:18). Prayer keeps believers connected to God's power and wisdom while fostering humility and dependence on Him.

Practical Advice for Discerning Truth from Error

Apostle Amor provides practical steps for identifying falsehoods using biblical principles:

1. **Test Every Spirit:**
   First John 4:1 advises Christians not to believe every spirit but test them against Scripture because many false prophets exist in the world. Any teaching or prophecy must align with God's revealed Word.

2. **Know Scripture Deeply:**

Psalm 119:105 describes God's Word as a lamp unto our feet—a guide through darkness. Regular study equips believers with knowledge needed for discernment.

3. **Examine Fruits:**
   In Matthew 7:16-20, Jesus teaches that true character is revealed by actions rather than appearances.[5] Good trees produce good fruit; likewise, genuine teachers exhibit godly behavior consistent with their message.

4. **Seek Wise Counsel:**
   Proverbs 11:14 highlights safety found in seeking counsel from mature Christians who possess wisdom rooted in Scripture.

5. **Rely on the Holy Spirit:**
   John 16:13 promises that the Holy Spirit guides believers into all truth. Through prayerful dependence on Him, Christians gain clarity amidst confusion.

Conclusion

In "Battling Deception – Standing Firm Against Falsehoods," Apostle Bill Amor calls readers to take up their spiritual armor daily while remaining grounded in biblical truth through study and prayerful reliance on God's guidance. By doing so faithfully over time—testing spirits carefully against Scripture—they can resist being led astray by false teachings or deceptive influences prevalent today just as they were during biblical times.

This chapter serves both as a warning against complacency regarding spiritual vigilance and an encouragement toward active engagement with God's Word so readers may confidently walk forward clothed fully prepared spiritually armored ready combat any form deceit encounter journey faith ultimately glorifying Lord Savior Christ Jesus eternity await faithful obedient children Almighty Father Creator Universe!

Chapter 11: Victory Through Christ – Overcoming Sin and Death

The resurrection of Jesus Christ is the cornerstone of the Christian faith, representing the ultimate victory over sin and death. This chapter celebrates that triumph, drawing from key passages in the King James Version (KJV) Bible to emphasize how believers can live victoriously through Christ. By understanding the significance of Jesus' resurrection and its implications for humanity, readers are encouraged to embrace a life of freedom, hope, and eternal joy.

The Consequences of Sin

The Bible makes it clear that sin has dire consequences. Romans 6:23 states: **"For the wages of sin is death; but the gift of God is eternal life through Jesus Christ our Lord."** This verse highlights two contrasting realities: the inevitability of death as a result of sin versus the promise of eternal life through Jesus Christ. Sin separates humanity from God, leading to spiritual death and eternal separation from His presence. However, God's love provides a way out—through His Son, Jesus Christ.

Paul's letter to the Romans explains that all have sinned and fallen short of God's glory (Romans 3:23).[2] Yet, through Christ's sacrificial death on the cross, believers are offered redemption. This act of grace underscores that salvation is not earned by human effort but is freely given by God as a gift.

The Power of Resurrection

Jesus' resurrection is central to overcoming sin and death. In 1 Corinthians 15:55-57, Paul exclaims: **"O death, where is thy sting? O grave, where is thy victory? The sting of death is sin; and the strength of sin is the law. But thanks be to God, which giveth us the victory through our Lord Jesus Christ."** These verses celebrate how Jesus conquered both physical and spiritual death by rising from the grave.

Through His resurrection, Jesus demonstrated His authority over all powers—including sin and Satan. Revelation 1:18 records Jesus declaring: **"I am he that liveth, and was dead; and behold, I am alive for evermore, Amen; and have the keys of hell and of death."** This statement affirms that Christ holds ultimate control over life and death itself.

Believers are invited to share in this victory. Romans 8:37 proclaims: **"Nay, in all these things we are more than conquerors through him that loved us."** By uniting with Christ in faith, Christians can overcome not only personal struggles with sin but also fear of death.

Living Victoriously in Christ

Victory through Christ calls for a transformed life—a life marked by freedom from sin's bondage. Romans 6:4 explains this transformation beautifully: **"Therefore we are buried with him by baptism into death: that like as**

Christ was raised up from the dead by the glory of the Father, even so we also should walk in newness of life." Baptism symbolizes dying to one's old sinful nature and being raised into a new existence empowered by God's Spirit.

Living victoriously means embracing this "newness of life." It involves daily surrendering to God's will (Luke 9:23), resisting temptation (James 4:7), and walking in obedience to His Word (Psalm 119:105). While challenges may arise, believers can take heart knowing they are not alone—Christ promises His presence always (Matthew 28:20).

Eternal Hope Beyond Death

One of Scripture's most comforting promises comes from Revelation 21:4: **"And God shall wipe away all tears from their eyes; and there shall be no more death, neither sorrow nor crying; neither shall there be any more pain: for the former things are passed away."** This verse paints a picture of ultimate restoration—a future where suffering ceases entirely because God has made all things new.

This hope empowers Christians to endure trials with confidence. As Paul writes in Philippians 3:20-21,[12] believers eagerly await their Savior who will transform their mortal bodies into glorious ones like His own. Such assurance enables them to face even life›s darkest moments without despair.

Conclusion

Victory over sin and death is not merely an abstract theological concept—it is a reality made possible through Jesus' resurrection. By accepting Him as Lord and Savior, believers receive forgiveness for their sins along with eternal life. They are no longer slaves to fear or condemnation but are free to live boldly as children of God (Romans 8:15-16).[13]

As Apostle Bill Amor emphasizes throughout his book "Be Child of Truth 'Who Are and Who Were' vs. Child of Lie 'Who Was and Now Is Not!'," living victoriously requires aligning oneself with God's truth while rejecting deception. Readers are encouraged not only to celebrate what Christ has accomplished but also actively participate in His victory by living lives characterized by faithfulness, gratitude, and unwavering hope.

Chapter 12: Eternal Destiny – Life or Death?

The final chapter of Apostle Bill Amor's book, *Be Child of Truth 'Who Are and Who Were' vs. Child of Lie 'Who Was and Now Is Not!'*, brings the reader to the ultimate question that every human being must face: What is your eternal destiny? This chapter explores the stark contrast between two eternal outcomes—eternal life with God or eternal separation from Him in hellfire. Drawing heavily from Revelation chapters 20-22 in the King James Version (KJV) Bible, this chapter serves as both a sobering warning and an urgent invitation to embrace Jesus Christ as Savior before it is too late.

The Great White Throne Judgment

Revelation 20 introduces readers to the climactic moment known as the Great White Throne Judgment. In Revelation 20:11-12, John writes:

"And I saw a great white throne, and him that sat on it, from whose face the earth and the heaven fled away; and there was found no place for them. And I saw the dead, small and great, stand before God; and the books were opened: and another book was opened, which is the book of life: and the dead were judged out of those things which were written in the books, according to their works."

This passage reveals that all humanity will one day stand before God to give an account of their lives. The "books" mentioned here represent records of every deed done during one's lifetime, while "the book of life" contains the names of those who have accepted Jesus Christ as their Savior. Those whose names are not found in this book face a terrifying fate described in Revelation 20:15:

"And whosoever was not found written in the book of life was cast into the lake of fire."

This judgment underscores that rejecting truth—rejecting Christ—leads to eternal separation from God.

Eternal Separation: The Lake of Fire

The Bible describes hell as a place of unimaginable torment. Revelation 21:8 provides a vivid description:

"But the fearful, and unbelieving, and the abominable, and murderers, and whoremongers, and sorcerers, and idolaters, and all liars, shall have their part in the lake which burneth with fire and brimstone: which is the second death."

This "second death" represents eternal separation from God—a state where there is no hope for redemption or relief. It is reserved for those who choose lies over truth by rejecting Jesus Christ. The inclusion of "all liars" in this list ties directly back to earlier themes in Apostle Amor's book about living as a child of lie versus a child of truth.

Hell is not merely a punishment but also a consequence—a natural result—of choosing to live apart from God's truth. As Proverbs 14:12 warns:

"There is a way which seemeth right unto a man, but the end thereof are the ways of death."

Eternal Life with God

In contrast to this grim reality stands an indescribably glorious promise for those who choose truth by accepting Jesus Christ. Revelation 21 paints a breathtaking picture of eternity with God:

"And I heard a great voice out of heaven saying, Behold, the tabernacle of God is with men, and he will dwell with them, and they shall be his people, and God himself shall be with them, and be their God. And God shall wipe away all tears from their eyes; and there shall be no more death, neither sorrow, nor crying, neither shall there be any more pain: for the former things are passed away." (Revelation 21:3-4)

This passage reveals that eternity with God is marked by perfect peace, joy, love, and communion with Him forever. There will be no more suffering or sin—only unbroken fellowship with our Creator.

Revelation 22 continues this vision by describing "a pure

river of water of life" flowing through "the holy city," where believers will reign forever (Revelation 22:1-5). This imagery reflects both spiritual abundance and eternal satisfaction found only in God's presence.

The Urgent Call to Choose

Apostle Amor concludes his book by emphasizing that each person has been given free will to choose their eternal destiny. Jesus Himself extends an open invitation in Revelation 22:17:

"And whosoever will let him take the water of life freely."[7]

This verse highlights God's desire for everyone to come to Him willingly—not out of compulsion but out of love. However, time is limited as Hebrews 9:27 reminds us:

"And as it is appointed unto men once to die but after this judgment."

The decision cannot be postponed indefinitely because no one knows when their earthly life will end.

Final Plea

The chapter ends with Apostle Amor urging readers not to

delay making this critical choice. He reiterates Jesus' words from John 14:6:

"I am the way—the truth—and—the life; no man cometh unto Father—but by me".

To reject Christ means choosing lies over truth—and ultimately forfeiting eternal life.

Will you choose truth or lies? Will you embrace Jesus Christ today while there's still time? Your eternal destiny depends on it!

Conclusion

Apostle Bill Amor's book, *"Be Child of Truth 'Who Are and Who Were' vs. Child of Lie 'Who Was and Now Is Not!'"*, serves as a profound reminder of the eternal choice every individual must make: to live as a child of truth, walking in God's light and embracing His eternal Word, or to fall into the fleeting deceptions of lies that lead to spiritual destruction. The Bible makes it clear that truth is not just an abstract concept but is embodied in Jesus Christ Himself (John 14:6). To be a "Child of Truth" means to abide in Him, live according to His Word, and reflect His character in our daily lives.

Conversely, the Bible warns against the dangers of deception and falsehood. Satan, described as "the father of lies" (John 8:44), seeks to lead people away from God's purpose through deceit. Revelation 17:11 reminds us that all lies and false powers are temporary and destined for destruction. Choosing truth over lies is not just about morality—it is about aligning oneself with God's eternal kingdom versus being separated from Him forever.

For those who may feel uncertain about their salvation or unsure whether they are living as a "Child of Truth," this book provides both encouragement and guidance rooted in Scripture. It challenges readers to examine their hearts, test their faith (2 Corinthians 13:5), and fully surrender to God's will so they may walk confidently in His truth.

Prayer for Those Uncertain About Their Salvation

Heavenly Father,
We come before You today with humble hearts, seeking Your guidance and assurance. Lord, Your Word tells us that You are the way, the truth, and the life (John 14:6), and no one comes to the Father except through You. For anyone reading this who feels uncertain about their salvation or unsure if they are truly walking as a "Child of Truth," I pray that You would reveal Yourself to them in a powerful way.

Father, Your Word promises that if we confess with our mouths that Jesus is Lord and believe in our hearts that You raised Him from the dead, we will be saved (Romans 10:9). Help those who are struggling with doubt to take this step of faith today. Let them know that Your love is unconditional and that salvation is not earned by works but given freely by grace through faith (Ephesians 2:8-9).

Lord, I ask that You open their eyes to see the beauty of Your truth and give them discernment to reject the lies of the enemy. Fill them with Your Holy Spirit so they may walk boldly in righteousness and reflect Your light in a dark world. Remind them that nothing can separate them from Your love—not fear, not doubt, not even past mistakes (Romans 8:38-39).

Thank You for being patient with us when we falter and for always calling us back into Your arms. May everyone reading this prayer find peace in knowing they are loved by You eternally. In Jesus' name we pray, Amen.

Apostle Bill Amor

About Apostle Bill Amor

Apostle Bill Amor's life is a testament to the power of faith, perseverance, and divine intervention. Diagnosed with autism as a child and considered high-functioning as an adult, Apostle Amor has faced challenges that would have broken many.

Born into a world that often misunderstood him, young Bill struggled with feelings of isolation and inadequacy. Despite these challenges, he displayed remarkable determination. At the age of 12, he achieved a significant milestone by winning a reading competition—an accomplishment that filled him with pride and optimism. However, this joy was short-lived when his mother tearfully shared devastating news from the doctor: he was not expected to live beyond the age of 28 to 32.

This revelation shattered his world. Overwhelmed by fear and hopelessness, Bill sought solace in his best friend John Straw, only to discover that John had been taken away by his brother Andy. Feeling abandoned and consumed by anger, he fled into the woods near his home. It was there, amidst the trees and shadows of doubt, that he cried out to God in desperation.

Bill's life changed forever on that fateful day. As he climbed a steep hill toward his neighbor's house, he encountered what can only be described as a divine vision: Jesus Christ Himself appeared before him at the top of the hill near a chain-link fence. The image was vivid—Jesus stood before him with pockmarks where His beard had been removed and glistening divots on His cheeks and chin. He did not resemble traditional depictions; instead, He appeared timeless yet distinct from modern trends.

This miraculous encounter marked the beginning of Apostle Amor's transformation. From a young boy who felt lost and unworthy, he grew into a man devoted to spreading God's message of love and repentance. Through trials and tribulations—including struggles with literacy—he found strength in faith and discovered his purpose as an apostle.

Apostle Amor's mission is clear: to guide others toward spiritual healing by sharing his testimony of divine grace. With humility born from hardship and wisdom gained through faith, he invites readers to embark on their own journeys toward repentance and renewal.